BURN AND DODGE

DATE DUE

PITT POETRY SERIES

Ed Ochester, Editor

BURN AND DODGE

SHARON DOLIN

UNIVERSITY OF PITTSBURGH PRESS

Published by the University of Pittsburgh Press, Pittsburgh, Pa., 15260
Copyright © 2008, Sharon Dolin
All rights reserved
Manufactured in the United States of America
Printed on acid-free paper
10 9 8 7 6 5 4 3 2 1
ISBN 13: 978-0-8229-6005-8
ISBN 10: 0-8229-6005-2

This book is the winner of the 2007 Donald Hall Prize in Poetry, awarded by
the Association of Writers and Writing Programs. AWP, a national organization
serving more than three hundred colleges and universities, has its headquarters
at George Mason University, Mail Stop 1E3, Fairfax, VA 22030.

E vidi spirti per la fiamma andando;
     per ch'io guardava a loro e a' miei passi,
     compartendo la vista a quando a quando.

And I saw spirits walking through flames,
     so that I watched them and my steps,
     my gaze divided—now here, now there.

—Dante, *Purgatorio* XXV, 124–26

Burn and Dodge: In photography, a pair of darkroom techniques: to burn is to overexpose, to dodge is to underexpose to the light.

CONTENTS

VI

I

TO GUILT

Eighth deadly sin, half-
    hidden dissembler you resemble
    dwarf centipede hunching
    among dead leaves and soil—or are you between Envy
who bites her nails and Sloth who can't be bothered?
    You vanish when I'm hard at work
    then gash me when I sit to read a novel or even think
    of running to the movies or out to buy a skirt.
Or else your stepsister Mother-Guilt with her 82 legs
    barges in on me here in the café
    when I think I've given you the slip;
    she finds me slacking off for five minutes
not with my child but reading the paper
    about a new species of centipede discovered
    in Central Park. How else assuage you but equate
    you draw you in: among leaf litter at less than half an inch
you are shorter than your name, *Nannarrup hoffmani*.
    With your poisonous fangs you will probably eat me
    when I am nothing but body; for now
    feed on this.

THE WANT ROOM

I want to unshroud my desire
    for desire, now that I've plumbed midlife
        where nothing nimbles the heart numbed,

so that the most I can do is long for longing, hanker
    for rank hunger, thirst for raw thirst.
        I want to kneel at the foot

of this desk, bed, door and pray
    I can still pray for something.
        That the blood and breath of this body

can still rise and pant for someone.
    That even if it's taken all day to unfold
        these few minutes accordioned in

before I snap on the body-
    suit of Mother, the Goodly
        Housewife at the sofa, the table, the range,

that the Want Room will still open for me
    with my blunted key: a yearning to turn
        in the welter, crash through the soundproofed,

blind look unstuck. That I can crave time
    for time, lust for lust, hope for
        hoping I awaken each day, wanting

to want.

REGRET

Here's another sin you're sunk within
owl-necked looking back
to where you might have been
or what you could have done
to keep you from the muck
you're stuck standing in.
The lover not kissed the one
you seem to miss
this tree not the one you want to see or shinny
you can't believe this skintight is your skin.
The road not taken was always
the one worth trying. But you didn't
think so back then only now
in constant replay
while you're stewing out here
on the highway thumbing
for your life.

THEY

They terrified us.

They were the gnarled roots of where her life was going or had gone—exposed.

They didn't keep her from walking—she barely walked anyway.

They were her yellowed ivory keys—unplayed—her twin sets of venomous
spears.
   (How did they ever fit inside her shoes?)

They were her rage hardened to a brittle clasp of curls. They were the last to stop
growing.

They were her Medusa ringlets of keratinized horn.

They were sirens of beetles; they clicked when she talked.

They were a plague on both her daughters.

They were so hard we soaked them before cutting them. They resprouted
overnight, insidious fungi in the rain.

They were the one ugly unforgivable thing about her.

They are what happens when a mind lets a body go.

SHAME

When my five-year-old, not listening, climbed over
    the broken fence head first

and fell (the gash on his cheek, a huge backward "C"),
    we didn't recognize, as he bled,

what he'd opened up for himself
    until the next morning at dawn

when he ghost-walked into my room
    as was his custom (to lie with me

or wake me)—only this time he stood himself
    face into the corner, face to the wall,

and said, *I want you to look at it.*
    Only my story—which his wound opened

up for me—seemed to comfort him:
    as though imagining his mother as a

six-year-old, nose-to-nose with a collie,
    while her friend, unbeknown to her,

pulled his tail while saying *Kiss Brandy,* though
    the dog lunged before I could

and fanged my upper lip and cheek, my son
    cheek-to-cheek with me

could hold his story up with mine and bear
    the shame of the gash, the stitches

or the fear of them, the stinging dab of ointment,
   the questions that are always

another gash—the one that never heals, that reopens
   and bleeds when asked.

GRUDGE

Holding—bearing—carrying.
To have is not to surrender
pockets of the mind
where hurt sojourns.

Slighted by the least
attention paid to another,
stunned by someone's blue rage,
or, at the least, betrayed,

lied to, not apologized to:
How many of these tales
do you exile beneath
your skin until you're

positively pouched—
squirrel-cheeked—
with griefs? No wonder
no one can get close to you

with all those layers of chagrin.
So easy, wasn't it, telling your
four-year-old: Forgive.
Raise clenched fists high

and let them go.

For you it's not so simple.
Admit you hold each insult in.
Know what you need to lose?
Not pounds. Wounds!

WANTING TWO: A SONNET/GHAZAL

Is the lightning zip, knotty rough
in your crotch not enough?

Molten multiplied to the nth
till you cry out Stop! Enough.

Band pouring on past four, you
slamming into bodies—hot enough?

Is turning to your partner pillowed, finding
all you've ever lain with—copped enough?

Is woodpecker to its tree, is you knee-
to-knee, groin-to-mouth—what's enough?

Is lion-son asleep in shade, is harte-
beest not flayed to rot enough?

Head upon breast, silk within rest, wanting
to return to desk: one's a lot—enough.

ENTREATY TO INDECISION

Anxiety's flunky—you do in your
    undoing her grunt work. Heart-flutterer, sleep-
    depriver it is to you—two-headed

turncoat I have offered up my life.
    Dun-colored peahen,
    why can't I oust you at last

from the roost of me?
    You know how to tempt me
    on the one hand with your lavender veils

on the other, with sea-green
    so I'm a swivel-
    headed spendthrift.

Or when two paths (or men)
    loom before me I stand there Medusa'd
    quivering on caffeine

until one—or both—dries up or grows over-
    grown with brush (or moves on)
    and so I plod, plod, plod

the one still left (or else bereft)
    always leaning toward / dreaming about
    the right one. Can't you stop?

I've worshiped at your twin altars long enough.
    Not to decide is to decide
    on my teenage wall my

postered boast to live by.
    Thirty years later you're in my blood
    and when your anxious mistress

wells up inside don't I know by now
     what I have to do to be rid of you?
     Or do I?

TO THE FAMILY OF THE MAN WE ATE
130 YEARS AGO

Nabutautau, Fiji

We are sorry, but when your kinsman, the reverend,
touched the head of our chief
    what else could we do?
The head you must know is the crown
where the spirit floats and
    his hand, which had touched so many
unclean things—his wife's body
with its many fluids and folds, his own
    body, a chicken's wing, even
patted a dog's back with it and then
he raised it to our chieftain's
    head to remove a wooden half
a fishbone—comb, he called it,
after he had shown him one gliding
    through his own hair—well—in
the rain we anointed him with oils
said our blessings and cooked him
    and ate him. His boots—we'd never
seen such things before—we cooked with *bele*
similar to your spinach but they were
    too tough. See here, we've kept them
for almost 130 years and now return them to you.
Now we offer you many whale's teeth—one
    for each year his spirit has been
wandering in our bellies—may he swim
to shore and stay with you.
    And may you lift this curse from us
that has kept us hungry all these years
with little outside light and very
    matted hair.

ENVY SPEAKS

As soon as Virtue is born, Envy comes to the world in
opposition to it, and sooner will the body be without
a shadow, than Virtue without Envy.
—LEONARDO DA VINCI

Behold me, I've got no shame.
    I'm a naked 500-year-old woman
        riding Death, saddled with a quiver of arrows.

Peel back my mask so, fevered, you'll
    writhe while I declaim,
        "The art of losing isn't hard to master."

Everyone courts me
    as my brighter half, Fame, who is turning
        her back on you. Watch me

shake my thick red curls at your stringy,
    greying flax. I'm coffee-colored;
        you're sallow-skinned, freckled,

and spider-veined. One glance at my face
    you'll gnash your teeth and steal off
        with my bad boy Rage

whose body ignites beside me each night.
    How can he sleep with you?
        If he draws too near, you'll be singed to ash.

Rack yourself knowing I'm your shadow-life:
    pouring brine on your sweets,
        leeching carnelian to broody grey.

But you can't take your eyes off me
    as I depart for La Scala
        to sing "Che cos'è Amor?"

or, Venus-turned, winning 40-Love at tennis;
    isn't it always my face covered in sweat,
        aged/ageless, you covet,

no matter how much it makes you seethe?

THE TRUTH OF POETRY

> if you demand on the one hand,
> the raw material of poetry in
> all its rawness and
> that which is on the other hand
> genuine, you are interested in poetry.
> —MARIANNE MOORE

At the Philadelphia Zoo, it is true I saw the Galapagos
    Tortoises copulating: his gigantic shell riding on top
of hers, his leathery neck
      straining out as far as it could in a tight erection of muscles, eyes
        bulging out; her head recessed, eyes
        lidded in the shell. They were

a pair of opposites—sculptural they were so still and all the human
    eyes upon them—so still. Yet if I don't tell who brought me over to
that brightly lit glass, would this
      real zoological garden have imaginary tortoises
        in them, would it remain a place
        for the genuine? Doesn't

the genuine include my niece, sixteen, with her new girlfriend, embracing
    watching rapt ("She looks like she doesn't like it.") who pulled me over
on the first day she came out?
      With my niece and her friend—I could see there would be no "on top of" no
                            strain-
      ing in to tap the moist egg but
      a lying beside, neck-to-

neck, or lips-to-lips. And what of the rawness? Doesn't it rely on their
    fascination (they stood at that window for twenty minutes)
      and my fascination for them?

CURRENT EVENTS

Bin Ali, a village elder in Butit Meranti,
lost everything except a white dish
when a raid left 36 houses in ashes.

1. WHO YOU

are, might have been / framer of your narrative:

inveterate cap-wearer, brow-furrower—
weakens the tie between proper

and name.

Your *were* whirrs inside the motor-motive *are*.

Action are you or memory-bundle
vicissitudes of others' longings

doesn't your pillow own you call you by

your secret name:

nomen   *nombre*   *nomina*
omen   *gnomon* . . .

When in Lisboa you sport a boa
board the yellow tram to the Baixa
to look for the ghost of Pessoa.

your name suffuses with suffixes: -son, -sky, -zweig, -traub

Do not ask for whom to tell unfolds:
It tells the self.
                 (It wields the wail [within the well])
It's hell to tell [for thee & me].
If I were you (and you are we)
displacement would hardly figure
in the feeling-swirl you're tempted to say
is who we be.

Westerner, you read obituaries of obscure inventors.
Indonesian, you wear a crowd. Or shroud.

Have you financed a massacre? Is your name a poster?

(Reporter / killed   peerless unpurled)

Or do you go nameless: mommy   nanny   taxi
driver—the news barely grazes you in the playground or car

unless you're blown to bits or saved from fire or the collapsed mine.

But *who* is the person to whom things happen

(scandal not a name but an outcome)

or to exclaim: *Who the devil   Who on earth*
                                                    has done what?

2. WHAT-KNOTS

What do you let in / what stays penned
    in the when of then. Bishops de-
    frocked or the body as bomb.

What is *that* which does
    and may have the force of *who*
    though deeds breach higher than names

as after the bombing remember
    those namelessly scouting for shreds
    of flesh and bone and teeth to be buried.

Or pitched in to private abouts
    the collocation of those with these:
    meals and showers / phone calls and teakettle

whistles punctuating the working hours
    pulling on shorts / fighting off dolor.
    Or do headlines sharpen the what:

Rebels   **Natural Gas**   **Bullet Holes**   **Ice Caps**

Unfrozen   **Caribou**   **Approaching the Mainland**

    Another Body Orbiting Jupiter

And what of cells hiding everywhere
    and separatist movements quelled.

If you look up *what*, will you find it insepar-
    able from *who* and *how*? Any *which*
    or *that* or *whatever.*

The most thinginess of interrogatives or
        if unheard *What?* suffices to summon
        back the teller and stay the listener:

In the debris of Mr. Bin's home,
        only a white porcelain serving dish,
        a present to his wife, survived intact.

White porcelain serving dish. Let that stand for *what:*
        the broken / the husband-to-wife bond /
        the rebels / the crackdown (in Aceh, Sumatra) /

the grief. What though the rose have hips
        yet is it inflamed   if not embossed.
        Let *what* beware

of *where.*

it's heating up. Or not. Under or over / outside
your window pounding cement and scaffolding.
In the mind's kitchen.
Heart's dressing room. In Berlin. It's
where you've been. Map of every place your feet
have sited. All the wheres happening
at once: dark when you're in light / Australian winter
when you're summering / death gasp / birth heave / even desire's
rave or leave (crave or peeve?). Not wherefore
which means why but the here and there that makes
you move or string up wires / satellites to talk
between. Today the suicide bomber hit
Patt Junction in south Jerusalem. Razor
wire / ditches / walls / sensors going up for 225 miles to separate Jew
from Arab so there is a here and over
there / a not here. Where is the reason
(almost) for every war. Call it Kashmir.
Call it Jerusalem. Texas. Call it
Basque. What is your where? Do you
sell wares there? Wear your hair covered
there? I claim the territory of your heart
your throat. Anywhere is not somewhere.
Nowhere is where you'll vanish in the when
of not yet. Be distant. Play in the other
where of elsewhere. Before you move into
back when.

4. WHEN, THEN

It was and then it wasn't. An hour
ago. Two days before. That split second
    boarding the bus. (It was just before 8 a.m.)
He looked like a terrorist in his red bulgy shirt
    when he didn't pay. Then he wasn't. Just
an exploding belt of ball bearings. Three women
    in frocks sitting there with their heads blown off.

    Why intrudes. *They want to see us dead.*
Now   now   now. Not now. Before you came.
    Before you were born. (Or he. Laughing with
the Boss at the cash machine before they crashed the plane tomorrow.)
    Mother at wounded boy's bedside while father's
home rejoicing when he hears his son was the bomber.
    This *when* ensnares *where.*

Beit Safafa refugee camp. Afterwards. The next day.
    A year later in Lower Manhattan (Towers burned,
legs crushed) she is still in hospital. And you, over morning tea
    mourning the morning of the day before.
They want to kill us in the when of every
    where. Cry of why. For Ishmael's cold tears? For the when of who
was there first? For Isaac's hoarse laugh? And for what
    kind of God?

5. AT WHEN

Three thirteen p.m. (mine)
    four fifty-nine p.m. (his from my between)
    To crown is not to frown

but a push to enter the gate of recorded time
    a look before knowing at
    what or whom

seven years: my books have been housed
    in this upper Mannahatta
    dream-cubby

eternity: my name for infinity
    (being barely ten)
making when and where collide/coincide
    in the beyond

Seven p.m.: cocktails—news—moon hour
    word-opening night / prayer-
    plant-foldings till dawn.

6. WHY AS IN

Wherefore. Motives.
Causes that produce
unasked-for effects. (*Who shall live . . .*)

As in reproach. Fist-
shaking at sky. At your lover-
other. Maker. (*Who shall die . . .*) Resist:

Why couldn't he have been   elsewhere?
For what reason did I have to lose you?
Paradigm of unanswerables.

As if thinking it through
pieced the puzzle / lessened the ire—
On account of which / in spite of   new

virus discovered. Or exiles' dream-desire.
Attaches to *who*. Emboldens *what*.
And where did she. And when. Never

back where you started
from. Secret cause. Works around
the kiss. Beetles brows.

Opens the oh-my-god mouth
into an afterimage of oh no . . . yes.
Editorials on the soul. Accounts

for wars and local turf skirmishes
in the sandbox, the West Bank.
Island no one wants

until the other side sends in tanks.
That's mine. My
Temple Mount. / My mosque.

Call it the key
to an unbuilt room
you discover—too late—

you may not enter   by asking.

7. AND HOW

By fire. By stammering. Stoning. By water.
By hook. By wandering. By the seat of.
By being there. By phone.
By election. At home. By the side
of. With butterflies. By rote.
By beating. Whisking. Tongue-
kissing. In furtive. In solitude.
Standing up. Crouching over her.
Looming over him. With your eyes
closed. With his big toe. With
the baby sleeping. While others turned
away. In groups of three. By leaning
against yonder tree.
By e-mail. In the lake. With
your jacket on. In the taxi. Not
in the backseat. With hope. Numbly.
Nimbly. Without stumbling. Drunk?
In between courses. Pushing really hard.
In the grass. Flat on your back.
With thumb and pointer. With your nose.
With know-how. With an acolyte.
With who?

8. HUH?

As in *What?* As in I don't get it. As in
emptied out but not refilled. As in
bower movements for headlines. You mean
who rests beneath? Or the hammock of
can't walk now. No coffee. No prison
is. No lime tree. Pissoir in the dawn hours.
Moody not the same as temperamental.

Someday the paper will be custom-fit
to us. But not the world.
Envelopes of ash. 20,000 body parts
found. One-fifth by sifting through
the Fish Kills Landfill. She has several
parts of him but wants more / as much
as will make him whole again as possible.

But without the breath / spirit / soul?

What remains—
more and more that is less and less
of him: ringed finger, troublesome tooth
that is just some truth. And after hours in the
after-hours while the inked paper is run
drying through the rollers isn't
her despair the white space

white night? Isn't that it? Huh?

9. FIRST WHY

> Why indeed? But once you start whying, there's no end to it.
> —D. H. LAWRENCE

Because it's morning and birdsong is picking out
the valley.

Because you don't know and there is
no answer.

Because if it had worked out the other
way you'd still ask.

Because you're here to
ask.

Because you're never late for work
except that day you were.

Because why is first / last /
exhausting / inexhaustible.

ODE TO TURBULENCE

What
did you expect
  with a three-year-old what did you expect
  married or single dipping
    into your Ligurian seacoast dream

once
alone twice—thrice—
  companioned but never exactly the
  right mix of solitude and
    coupling nature's nature is thorny / face-

slap
-ping wave you have
  swallowed so with mouth salty eyes stinging
  you struggle to stay afloat
    while below—below—schools of black fish are

sus-
pended as though
  in a calm pond you may never enter
  it is here on the surface
    you lose everything to gain mastery of

your
wish for mastery
  you may not swim in the Bay of Silence
  or Bay of Fables only
    out here between this rocky outcropping

in
the noon hour where
  foam curtains furl over rock and gulls perch
  on cliffs above you biding
    their time—reminding you *you* cannot glide.

ODE TO MRS. MEUNIER, CAPTAIN OF THE GUARD, P.S. 119, BROOKLYN

What makes me think of you now after forty years of being
    quit of you?
Is it because you taught me Fear itself—with your lockjaw mouth,
    Furies' scream
I knew I'd die if ever I was subject to? Or because your lesson/
    master rules
the mistress of the law my parents never taught me you taught
    me how to quake
all night into the following day in my seat terrified of being
    reported to you
(I never was, why wasn't I) for that stolen touch my seven-year-old fingers
    couldn't stop themselves
from grazing the surface of the moon (soft or hard?) all dark
    grey-green clay
I'll never forget it (in between): the student guard hurrying over to take down
    my name. My
joy. My life.

GHAZAL WITHOUT THE MAN

You started out gangly, wrangling without the man.
Now you can't remember angling without the man.

Winter of frozen cherries matted in his beard,
Spring buds in hair tangling without the man.

Go. Drive a car, the weather wanders you.
Life's a zoo, stroke pangolin without the man.

Flux redux, can't undo. No mournful piccolos.
Such stuff as we are: Philandering without the man?

In Berkeley women loved women, men themselves.
Hard to play it straight, gamboling without the man.

Books inscribed, kisses under sheets—lost things landslide.
Oh, turn not morose, memories dangling without the man.

What if, after all is bled and flung, it won't add up?
Don't be so sure you can handle it without the man.

Sleepwalking roofs—you never were that sort.
Picked up, the pieces mangling without the man.

Got floaters in the eyes, water on the knees.
Getting older—still newfangling without the man.

Adrift yet moored, unfocused—is this how it'll end:
Your name's spelled *mandolin* without the *man*.

BARBAROUS THING

(after Amelia Roselli, pace Milton)

The sonnet is a barbarous thing. Intractable.
Short. With a door that swings (without wings).
Don't come in. Tiger unstriped the claw from which—
not a comfortable thing. Collapses within
as you doze on its waterbed skin.
Barb from the coast it throws you, barbate
it hides less-than-half its face. (A bearded
lady? Not exactly.) Never quiet *environs me*
of owls and cuckoos—stammers baba
bababa home to Berbers and Babar
who bought trousers to promenade
the boulevard as did asses, apes and dogs.
It has put on weight. Not Borzoi. Barks
barbarismos: Care to hear the way I mangle you

together?

O INDIGO

deep blue inclining to purple O see India, Greek *Indikos*

derivative indole subsidiary indolin
suggesting a loose blend of indigo plus aniline

brought to Europe by Levantine Jews
Egyptian mummy cases dyed with you

now farmed on Shikoku Island
few Japanese have the knees
for crouching all day over dye vats
of fermented leaves / lye / wheat bran / sake
with offerings to Aizen Shin

will you too disappear as did woad-blue for you
madder-red receding to indole?

yet being born in dolin inclining to indolent no wonder
I am deep blue that I am in dolin (last lass, alas)
can only kneel irregularly dipping self-threads in dye I
don't wear the wares just soak

and pull out indigo throat-scarves
without mordant first dipped comes out green minutes
tick to indelible blue

can take ten days for cloth to become peacock-breasted

obi kimono / my key moan O, O Be.

THE POEM FOR ENVY I CANNOT WRITE

will have to be written by somebody else
    the one I'd rather have been
who would have no trouble

sitting at her desk beneath its tilted green lampshade
    or in this orange-lollipop subway seat
to find the words to blunt Envy's sting. What if

I praise the thorns on the fire-tipped
    yellow rose of the man
who has just plunked down opposite

or the Death skull on the navy sweatshirt
    of the next man to sit there
or the quick grace of the woman (in her minister's collar!)

who stooped to retrieve the pencil
    I didn't notice dropping?
And if this is becoming an ode to Chance

perhaps that will cast the spell
    so Envy feels quelled enough to go
churn someone else's stomach keep

someone else up half the night.
    "You will have luck in everything
you turn your hands to do," says my Chinese fortune.

If that's true, instead of leaving Envy offerings
    should I be praising Lady Fortune
who rises up from her clamshell

cookie with her cheek always turned half
    away, her prophetic fickle-colored skirts gliding her
out of the room?

SONNET/GHAZAL TO SLEEP

These white nights she lacked sleep, she said.
How else conjure without black sleep, she said.

You hear the rushing cauldron-ear, sore throat;
How will it bring you near? Hack sleep, she said.

Worried pieces of the day replay: could have, should have.
If you're broken into bits how track sleep, she said.

Rome's Tevere already light, dividing art from heart;
Early and earlier hemisphere; why attack sleep, she said.

No nights, no morning star. You sit, a pool of light,
Inside the hum of where you are: Crack, weep, she said.

Forget all hand-me-down words of woe; even *oh no.*
Hissing addicts who like you, Flak sleep, she said.

Tomorrow is today, the border porous, Sharon a plain;
Before dawn, lie down, go back to sleep, she said.

AT THE RECEPTION, 1963

for Marianne Moore

There you are with your tri-
     cornered
          hat tipped way back /
a female Paul Revere with the beacon
of your eye

as you sit primly in
     a skirt
          suit the carna-
tion in your lapel beginning to droop
the teacup

and saucer perched on a
     napkin
          that rides atop
your black purse. (Isn't that what your poems did /
cheek-by-jowl

water-clear crystal be-
     side the
          scientist and
the aye aye leading to the bell boy with
the buoy ball?)

You're wearing support hose,
     loafers
          your throat gone as
wrinkly as a chicken neck, your eyes a
sad turtle's

your silk blouse tied with a
     bow you
          don't look a bit

like Fangs or Rat except you scavenged for
your poems:

pack-rat's treasury rag-
    picker's
        loot of table
scraps mixed with pearls from your reading journal.
Your pursed lips

are about to say some-
    thing you
        look right at the
camera right through time to where I sit
hatless in

loose pants wearing a ski-
    boot to
        support my bro-
ken foot a cane beside me a puppy
asleep on

my thigh. What is it a-
    bout your
        gaze so that I
feel snapped by you / all the generations
you knew and

did not know about to
    raise your
        cup to them as
I am about to raise my cup to you.
It is a

smile of satiety
    that says:
               I have endured
despite the parties the receptions the
ball games the

snapshots. You will endure
    despite
        these encounters
and the dark hours at your desk because the
syllable

endures and as long as
    we can
        count you can count
on that.

ODE TO GINGER

Horn-shaped body, Srnga-vera,
　　from the tropics of South Asia
　　　　I have never beheld
your greeny flowers
　　only your tan potbelly
　　　　with its many stunted appendages.
You have rooted out my pain before:
　　when my wrists
　　　　and fingers throbbed
from too much
　　fluting of
　　　　lettered keys
I turned to you—
　　sliced and boiled in water—
　　　　plunged my hands in the pot
up to my wrists
　　among your bobbling chunks
　　　　as hot as I could stand.
Scalding drawing out
　　cricks and creaks
　　　　aches with your thousand needle-stings
into wet fire.
　　Now, when I have need
　　　　of fruit and lute
what else can lift me
　　into song but carrots—
　　　　sweetest firmest of ruddy roots—
and you, ginger, with your pungence—juiced—
　　whose burning cools the blood.
　　　　I'll drink up now
so impinging griefs, raging despairs, all
　　muddling worries
　　　　might hit your rapids
in their long blue craft
　　and singe themselves
　　　　out of me.

Here is why I am not Lynn Emanuel. And you know I wish I could be
Lynn Emanuel with her fast-talking ventriloquism, first she's not (for
spite) Sylvia Plath then she's not Emily Dickinson but one narrow room
then by god she is Gertrude Stein which feels like having swallowed
an ocean liner that can type and then she is Walt Whitman or after
becoming a waitress in Dacron Walt Whitman is she. So who's left for
me not to be but Lynn Emanuel. We're caught in that ecstatic embrace
of writer and reader that she and her Walt (perhaps you too, oh reader)
know so well. She is the writer

and I am the reader and you can tell I'm trying to switch roles but it's
not working so well, I feel like I'm learning Raoul's dance steps while
on the dance floor; now I'm leading but I'm really still following her
lead. And even if I am getting Raoul into this poem it's still her Raoul,
her lit window in the attic of her mind I can see inside of but can't quite
inhabit. I'm just too slow, too much the student; the top of my head
came off years ago at the Hotel Fiesta. Who am I kidding? We both
have our Bella Roma though I never modeled there—only as a mere
child before I had breasts or stockings or barely said "yes."

Because she is the paragon of brains and beauty and I am its epigone,
its wannabe. Its paragon of epigones and I have to look these words up
to make sure I am getting it right (isn't English amazing, by the way,
how we keep having to learn it?) and yes, I do mean Lynn Emanuel
is the "peerless example," the "unflawed diamond," "the very large
spherical pearl," but "the type size of 20 points"? No. Go back. She's
not that kind of paragon. The peerless pearl, yes. The diamond, okay.
And who am I? I'm the "follower," from the Greek epigonos meaning
"born after" as the sons of the seven against Thebes. But I've never

fought at Thebes. Nor did my father. But Lynn Emanuel's father did.
And she has, I'm sure of it. Lynn Emanuel has fought at Thebes. But
do I even know Raoul, let alone Emily or Walt or Gertrude, on a first-
name basis? And if I did become her wouldn't she be writing this (or

maybe she gave up and this is one of her rejects, one of the poems Lynn Emanuel threw away, called "On Sharon Dolin Not Being Lynn Emanuel"—she's already got one about not being Sharon Stone—and I've just plucked it from her trash—she does recycle.) Now, since I have failed to become her (or has she refused to become me?), I must confess I have never

described the draperies in the room of a poem (forget burnt orange). But I fear if I don't at least say I like draperies for the way you can pull them aside for more light, more of a view, I would be misleading you and her—and I do like light and so, I think, does Lynn Emanuel, even if it means she has to dig herself out of the Jerusalem dirt and watch as her bones are being reassembled. And I have to salute her, this Lynn Emanuel, I mean you, now that my failed ventriloquism is reaching its end (and aren't you glad, oh true readers, oh *vrai audience*), in a moment of surgery never-before-performed-on-the-literary-page,

for we are only joined at the mind (and then just barely), when I stop speaking we are severed, this botched suture, this you-and-I, this Lynn-and-I. Now I am vanishing so *Then, Suddenly* Lynn Emanuel may truly appear.

ODE TO FERNANDO PESSOA

from *Álvaro de Campos*

Ah, dolorous lucid grand limpid electrical fabricator.
Tensile-fevered scribbler.
Scribble, arranging our identities to part with distant bells
For a distant bell, totally concealed, antagonizes.

Who wrote us, who engineers us, grrrrowwwl eternal!
Oh for trespassing retinal mechanisms in fury!
I'm fury far out and within,
For all my selves—nervous desiccated forest,
For all of us—pupils for a day to come to quays where you sit!
Take hold of us with dry lips or grand rude modern horns.

You gave us our beard amazingly of pearl,
Gave expression to all of us minus sensation,
Like excessive contemporaneous divas or maquettes.

I'm feverish in hand—motorized like tropical Nature—
Randy as tropical humans—day ferry and fog and forcible—
Can't do, can do presently, bang tambourine or
Past be our future,
Pork or pheasant, his is to add or peasant.

He has platonic and virginal entrails deluding us electrical.
Soporific aurora, he's a human forum, a Virgil and Plato,
He peddles to Alexander the Great, to a secular Talmud sins quaintly.
Adam's cave of tears,
Cerebral escalator to secular seeming,
A damper ecstasy curries transmission for these symbols are volunteers,
Rouging, raging, cheering, struggling, ferrying,
Fashion me an excess of caresses oh numinous corporeal caress of elms.

Ah, power, express me like a motor-sex in prime!
Complete me like mama can, ah!

Pose derriere (not vital), triumphant like a late-model car!
Pose me not penetrate me physically of all you are,
Raise, guard me to do . . . ah, briar me completely.
Doses of perfume, or layered or lured and carved
Destined to floral stupendous, black, artificial and insatiable!

Alas, ruin us, alas break us, hell ho la foule!
To do or keep as "to do or keep jasmine mountains!"
Commerce; invaders; crooks exaggeratedly well-dressed;
Members evidently of aristocratic clubs;
Squalid figures too biased; family chefs vaguely for lease
And paternity not current, hearing it traversed. Oh
Call it day algebra . . . ah algebra!
All passes, all that passes and never passes!
Presence emaciated accentuated does cook us!
Banality interesting (and can a sage keep her indentured?)
Dazed bourgeois, may he fill her generously,
A feminine grace is false to those pederasts that pass lean-tos;
And today the simplest of gents elegantly
Capers and sequesters himself.
He finally tunes-almost-your labyrinth.
Ah, come, you desire sere or satin, near-distant total.

Oh fashion us mountains! Oh mannequins! Oh ultimate figurines!
Oh arty girls in utero cater to a gent that can compare!
Oh the grand Amazons come vying sexually!
Oh the electric announcers gave him a stare and he disappeared!
Oh lactating comes like a blue-jay, construes he is different.
Hey, cemetery, our mother, cement baton, new voice processors!
Progress equals armaments gloriously mortified!
Cure us, as canoes, metal-haters, submariners, airplanes!

Ah, move us totally, attitude: calm an affair.
Ah move us carnivorously,

Minor voice and vista, or coitus grande, banal, you tease
Oh coitus totally modern
Oh minors contemporaneous, form—actual and proximate—
Does his system immediately calm the Universe!
Now revel, a cow metallic, dynamic, deistic!

Up the whole jokeway, haste to the Derby,
Murder enters dentists until you capture dust! (Chorus:
A certain alto could enter through nonhuman portals!
And the old harem mimes:
"Alas, alas, alas, cat and dry!
Geisha me, porter a cab, inside encounter us, voices, sequin us."
"Hey, Sir Levantine," "do da rude chicken of blood.")
Seems no one savors them a sou!

Oh feral waves, oh aluminum old champions of feral ululators!
Oh keys, oh ports, oh come boys, oh "gwan in da states," "oh revoke all doors!"

Oh moment truncated like a foggy road,
Oh moment of striding rude men, noisy and mechanical,
Oh moment dynamical passing him to dance as bacchantes.
So fair and so bronze baby dares a dosie-do with eyes.

No one says "I exist au-pair." Jeered, derided, engender me.
Encat me in all our combinations.
Eye me in all our skies.
Gee, our general does helixes with all our natives.

Gull, gar, like all porcelain similitudes! Hoopla!
Ah, no. Sere us today apart!
Oh no sir. You today are a gent and today's a party!

YOUR ONLY MUSIC: SONNET/GHAZAL STARTING WITH A LINE FROM KEATS

There is nothing stable in the world; uproar's your only music.
In the middle of your life you know never to ignore your only music.

Why do you roam, restless, to Rome, or swim the sea at Lerici,
or, dreaming, ascend the Buddha terraces so Borobudur's your only music?

What you cannot hold, let go—or die. When the poet, estranged, killed herself
and child: to be or not to be the scorned of Elsinore's her only music.

You say you want to live more lives? Strive, first, to live your own.
When your flamenco heart stops, gored matador's your only music.

August, you trade car-tumult for windy thunder on the lake;
when you return to blaring asphalt, recall loon lore's your only music.

It takes your whole life to sing the dialect of your skin (not kin);
If you get caught in the labyrinth of ought, Minotaur's your only music.

To expiate your sins, shuckle as you pray on High Holy Days;
At the head of the year, Simah, *Baruch Atah's* your only music.

TAI CHI IN FOG

Bejeweled with dew   not a cobweb when you

look closely enough   between the bench legs

radial lines   a web with its ovular

bull's eye then turning   there's another and another

gnat caught in the labyrinthine   filaments entranced as you are

when you face the fog the hushed   oblivion of the lake

and a wooden float as if on mist   So this is how you might be tempted

to put your foot over the edge and walk on air-   like-water.

            The fog has its own fibers.

You can almost reach the unseen   shore with your will you pull back

prepare for your arms to   float up

CLARE-HEWN

> While in the juicy corn the hidden quail
> Cries "wet my foot" and, hid as thoughts unborn,
> The fairy-like and seldom-seen land-rail
> Utters "craik craik" like voices underground
>
> —JOHN CLARE

The dourest window, pheasant moon-in-phase,
We brave, while songsters in a mulish haze squire
Home these nippled fields and by their thighs
Of thistle, would, weary, herd our eyes.
End the reach; haggard, throwing hisses, stolen, we'll
Otherwise bruise when wrists re-steel.
Now let us calm the sense of flotsam being
What orders the panting reach of jeans
Sent twitching in bistro throngs, regales
Lewd hums, the jigs—our own—yell, spill what ails.
Our hearts, doused, toss mullein in their plaids
And often strand the stronger sons they had.
Midlover, jetsam reddens, thorned tonight;
Estranged, send it summer-swarmed, by eel-light.

A missed tea, that piece of, to say, Off, *grief*.
We all come, by turns meretricious, to someone's wry relief.
Tangled wit, the *ought* of risible tea lay,
Aspiring to forswear, regretful knees sway.
I blanket or regret, fall to knees (that oldest knot):
To see—and to have been seen—and then seen not.
Eyeing behooves, else glower sense, he vents
At me for rejoining in *jaws*, summer prying.
Ear-moist, diving highest, I ease a taller thicket,
Announce Time's sick of us, foam in its spigot.
Handmaids mate in teal water (know they're not);
Handsome sires rush thither, upbraid, forged knot.
Cool delay, seeing anhedonian repast,
Too *they*, at fault, and die; lie calm, moon madder atlas.

Their son had stunned his wayward mouth to wince:
Little wily sniveler sulking for a chance-
Win from the hazarding world despised.
The I (vied, gainsaid by the past or sighed)
Lunged, hidden, sought a fox not in the glade.
Word-somnolent, let them rest in shade
When turned bye-byers and bruised by assiduous thanks,
Wheel-hefted he (why wouldn't they) which on cliff-verge sank.
Shirt off, swore, passed his grin around—surfeited now—
To glower, not be, nor weary, of the found hound
(Rear paw burr-draggled, fell with howl-hour).
The showered din he fled, slept up in peaceful tower.
Ends afraid, mules his feet slipped in, he frowned.
Now that Time's unwarped, where has the woof unwound?

4. AN IDEAL LURE

Sun-treeing, a tease, I of ten loves took leave
Or held vigils, moored sea-brood for pillow.
Woe's ripe swill thoroughly reeks of skunk filigree
Like hapless pie-shovelers mewling as they chew
And marbled, the stunned sky diminishes the beach.
Turned beekeeper on the berry hives of breath
And on the brink sea droves in blooming reach
Their sting's what's in the way of hot death
Wriggled out of smoke-stops ashed, upend their swarm
By cattails punking from the steaming marsh
While lilies moor their roots their shoreward home
And rebel to the very cusp in garish
Juiced light they whirl, summer's tribe and fathom
While otters writhe, heaving from the bottom.

Missed hummer's restive ripped nest to the ear
Off his tree and picked your asking hand
Tenting the mount, tainted with Lucifer.
Bear-climate tizziness—where rushing by he stands
Erred brisk-neck, admits sense-derangement near:
Like, I was in pearly throes, day were as a mile,
This sticky greed asking a humless drum
Of tearing up my face—will blunder-stand?
Swifts swell, hum used to reach him—hell to fail.
In mallow, groans the drinker, chugs that ale,
The floodman tuning up the whorish soul
And hell at least lure-listens everywhere.
So scried, replies, *I should've wailed, deranged guesses.*
End quiet minds as smoke burns in your tresses.

This now false step for us lies all as one:
The boy crows testy, throws Frisbee at our heads.
Now thinks, *A paw's on fire,* and his rise is back;
The give, seek look is handsome, he chucks us,
And eeks his squeals in *Can't!* and has a fit.
Beggars eating, he, on which bracken weighs the wind?
Then busses close, with now likeable arm:
His stinting mother rousts him in the cold
And the half-arrested dog growls low and robs
The hen felled, to eat tooth-and-throng and goes aloaf-
ing. What? Chews the whelp? Better not with bittern spar:
The more vying thief, the more he'll throw his sway.
Teases sad-lib—a posture to the peace,
Awry, (father-groan), protested ease.

Isle of uneven tides to crawl along
Dowel arrowed knees orange with daisy strewn
Where foam the long reeds under sea, the sail
Jets back creel, out spouts this time-lorn
Eye to mussels or meet minnows newly spawned
Where they ring, grasping earth from these outré years
Where weary be-pined pond with sand, wordy children
Invent for flow, ere ballooned but now leap there
While in the jousting yawn the hidden krill
Circle wet my feet that hid as though unmoored.
The ferry, I like, and sailing see land roil
You turn, *Creek, creek,* tuck vices under ours
Greed lands (and sloth) to me (the ever undone, why toil),
And seethes, light fits into glimpse, a wound (unsound).

8. HER AT PLAY

Burst oregano between the toes splints her
And sleep, lip-antic, in reach enfolds her.
An undeterred widow's grief-grey bout
Like tall avenues of trees in storm: the fallen pout.
Time admires her hair blown high forswears
(Lame roan to thirst and prance and bray), mares
Hobble in the green by hazelnuts detoured
As from vines do fall the whorlèd gourd.
Thinned out, the sprouted grain runs in the mill.
Tumbling she still may dance the yearly reel
Giggle at their jokes and strut them in the fields.
Drawl they, *Well, tow'rd faintin' baths it's numbin' her.*
Shudders she, awakened fire—incense her bitter mirror.

Eyeing, vying, we're felly in a glide of spokes.
In the grey world far from being better yoked
Among the vultures and owly-fed,
We vied—every hearer grazing, fled.
Injured by strike and hard slip-stones, a child
Raced with only steep-threaded wiles;
Sighted, or bid pastures honest betrayed
With plighted felt the sinking bay unbuoyed.
Sought the nave miles out and hid under wheels
As whelm through whelks, though a child in heels,
The mob derided and flocked at those morose—
An easy fop in the world's extant rose.
The vying environed set lingering on the son,
On the grey wife and whisked self off alone.

10. THIS SCABBARD'S FREE

You—thigh-armed—rifted trunks all knotted,
Licensed to war's disdain on this tiny isle of scabbard,
Tooth-tetched, tending sun-shaded swart
And hearty love of myrtle leaves above,
Orion, sky-arrested ruse to sigh and lunge
In careless acts, rude and very flecked
With ticks on deer and dear ones that have run.
Home to stowaways new-wallowed in expect-
ed isle that bower your eyes in strung boughs,
You ring the solar vanishing magicians
And witches (life so hid behind mythic know-how)
Thaw that infernal spell, those incantations
Humdrum; few torpors brew in the mind
To weave some figment of itself behind.

V

CULLET

Ugly fish of a word   for the hardened beauty   blown neck
    of what gets thrown away   refused.
        Then taken up in a pocket   given away. Treasured
           in a velvet drawstring pouch. Utterly useless. Like memory.
      Memory's fixative.   Scrap.   Discard. Black
    as some waters (though not Venice's canals).
Fat bauble   headless
    fertility goddess   gold paint
      drizzled diagonal
         down one side. Rough
      spot to the touch could even cut skin
    where it was twisted off in fire.
Heavy in the hand
    and in the pocket to carry as the German father on the local vaporetto
      must have felt watching his young daughter
         befriended by a mother and son in English making a bridge
      of chatter all the way from the Rialto to the Giardino where we parted
    in search of a child's swing.
Reflective enough to see (did I mention?)
    the lamp lighting my peering in so that writing this
      I stand outside and within. Recall his smile,
        hand in pocket, composing something:
      loquacious American mother and child—his Venetian tale—
    just as he and the girl
and the broken-off piece he gave us—ours.

CLOAKROOM WIT

a perfectly good English phrase, she jactated, for what I
    called *esprit d'escalier*

      as she admitted to saying stupid things in the poetry foyer,
        so mock-regretful

        (her new book almost out), when it is to her viper
          tongue about my hair

          and face I've most rehearsed such afterthought retorts:
            Do you work at being nasty or were you born to sting.

            I've descended many stairs neck stung, head thrown back,
              have yet to enter

              a cloakroom since public school where I could hear
                among our pegged woolen coats

                the boys being hit.
                Some wit.

A PACT WITH EZRA POUND

252 Calle Querini

I make a pact with you, Ezra Pound—
here in the Dorsoduro after, yes, I admit it,
peering in the mail slot of the house you lived in
with Olga Rudge, and glimpsing
(near the peeling plaster)
a portrait of you still hanging by the fireplace.
I have hated your anti-Semitism long enough.
Nearby the graffiti screams along the Riva Fondamenta
morte a Israele / libera Palestina.
So your intolerance continues
(can I tolerate it?) amid so much beauty;
you lived on an alleyway of stone.
I come to you as a mother and a Jew
who has otherwise prized your lines.
Two steps away in the canal—
a gondola with a green crocodile on its side.
Children in red life vests are learning
the Venetian art of rowing.
Let me take it for a sign—
What thou lovest well remains,
      the rest let rest.

PASSING

on the elevator down with her dad, the blonde
    baby girl careens out full kilter.
        On another day she nimbles

alongside her mom whose face wears a permanent tan
    and freckles as she strolls
        beside her dark-skinned mom

in a generational parade, so I can't help marveling
    at the quick progress of lightening
        from grandmother to grandchild

and wondering: What will Ruby (for that's the little girl's
    name) call herself when she goes to check
        the boxes all of us must fill?

And you probably don't think it's the same (do you?)
    when I hesitate each time I check
        Caucasian, of European descent—

that I, too, am passing, in hiding with my -sky
    clipped off so I sport an Irish surname
        with straight blonde hair, blue-green eyes, snub nose.

That even the rabbis have always believed I must be a convert.
    In Brooklyn, fifty years after the Holocaust,
        in my Italian working-class neighborhood,

I never could bring myself to light
    a menorah in the window.
        One Saturday morning, when I descended

three flights from my walkup in a spring skirt,
    the worker who swept the walkway looked up,
        Where are you going all dressed up?

What I tossed off I'm no longer
    ashamed to say was true
        and also a cover,

for a voice inside whispered, Don't tell him
    you're going to synagogue,
        where it doesn't matter that Jews

(ask yourself what you think)
    are never quite white enough:
        I'm going to meet someone,

I said in passing.

SLATCH

so-called lull between the crash
    of waves / the moment to set hull
to sea heave-ho before the storm
    starts up again (as in some form it does)
before voices depart / faces gone slack / Clotho
    spun, Atropos took back. Now they rise
from this morning's slatch / photos give the lie
    beaming Mom still holds the swaddled
child / Judith's still gabbing at Moosewood
    over lunch (before she lost her hair) /
Billy the goat boy you nearly wed squints
    reclining on elbows on a Jamaican skiff,
biting his lower lip in a wounded smile
    that gives everything away.

JEALOUSY

Even after it had been over for years
and we'd both returned—somehow—
    to the same small town—Ithaca, it had to be—
and you were living with someone else
and I was just visiting, keeping
    company with a friend of yours—another architect—
one night he and I both ended up sleeping
on your living room floor, which you had offered us,
    and it struck me as only a bit awkward
for this was a time of floating for me
and I was grateful for any place to stay.
    When you walked out in the morning and saw
that we'd not only slept side-by-side
but slept together, your tear-stained
    fury stunned me
as it must have stunned your girlfriend
(she never came out of the bedroom)
    and you threw us both out (your friend and me)
hurling names and clothes and then it came back
why I'd left you years before—that raging
    possessiveness I could never stand—
the way, unasked, you used to rearrange
my living room furniture. And this all happened
    twenty years ago, before I heard
you had moved to Kentucky
and I moved back to New York
    and I haven't seen you since.

FORMS OF ADDRESS

After seven years write *him*   instead of *you*,
nine years still   call *you* not *her*
as though you   might answer.
No wonder baby says   first words to self & mom.
Echo chamber   we resound within
keeps going for life & after   one day you don't respond
one day I won't or replies   assume the shape of pigeon coos
     flying in & out of a sunny light well.
Does writing *him* mean the bones   have been picked clean, no more
contentious wrestling? There let him lie   as in life he lied about
his whereabouts and doings till   we caught him
being subterranean: shower left running
snaps I got handed   held fishnet
     embarrassments   I scissored in
among the kitchen scraps   gulls and rats picked clean left
     only filmy snips   (of her not me).
Though you too are surely free of   skin you held me in
why do you last?   Is it because I will not let you go
my first embrace, speech-target   huge & wavery-faced mirror
mutter-tonguing you   a way to hold on
though you be nothing but   a hovering?

ENVY GHAZALED

> O envy, root of infinite evils and woodworm of virtues!
> All vices, Sancho, bring with them some kind of delight, but
> envy brings nothing but vexation, rancor, and rage.
> —MIGUEL DE CERVANTES

Hydra-headed, you. No Heracles, I am being slain.
No wonder my favorite color is green—slain.

To slay you I slay myself: Mirrors dilate.
Looking at you I will be last seen slain.

Comparisons caper through my head in bed at night.
Why haven't I scaled the Apennines? Slain.

How many parts of lives I'd exchange: job, book, prize . . .
Emotional landmines at a party? Preen, slain.

Her coat, her house, her love, her life, her reputation.
Did I hear someone's off to the Mediterranean? Slain.

How to slay the heads inside without them
growing back to poison my sheen: Slain.

Sometimes you're my younger self: Self-envy
no oxymoron—nor envy of being nineteen: Slain.

Count me happy when I can enjoy the lot I've been given.
Confessing to you, I know it's quite obscene. Slain.

Write to exorcise—or exercise—you with lines, images, rhyme.
If Sharon does not from Envy wean—slain.

I HAVE

> I have cut bamboo:
> for you, my son,
> I have lived.
> —PAUL CELAN

I have cut time
for you, my son,
I have sliced hours

thin as mid-
night butter in our
predawn

tent
dark sentinel.

I did not choose it: you
can't remember those wind-
owed hours—all-night
diner lights our
cigarette ember

burning up
the dark
hovering roseate dawn
woke wake-
fulness.

DOOR LITOTES

Not ugly, really, off-white gone grey with pencil
    scratches made upon it.

Not too short, *You grew-some,* the father chuckled
    chucked her chin each time

scoring the new highest mark
    her head reached: language

of measure not a bad way to compress
    years into one space:

superimposed height of twenty- over sixteen-
    over twelve-year-old.

I'd like to take the door with us
    when we move, noticing the never-

been-painted graph not without aesthetic
    value: conceptual before conceptual art.

No longer a girl's body but a mother's: not so sad
    to become a door after letting in seed pushing

out the hatched cry. Once knee-to-heel was finger-length
    then finger to wrist, now not so small

(nearly three) well past her knee he almost grazes her navel, standing—
    not bad, being a breathing flesh-and-bone measuring door, not bad

at all.

UNCENTERED @ THE CATHEDRAL ROSE GARDEN

(Anxious still and almost missing it)
in buttercup light

(but not allowing quite the thing to pass)
given names like New Face, Ballerina

(my son & I)
Penelope, Perdita, Sceptr'd Isle

(bow heads into the candied blooms)
early morning even two peacocks are roosting

(though the next morning outside one turned his back)
and we have to peer up at them

(and spread his lush-eyed tail kept rotating)
in shadow

(away as though he found us unworthy)
to try and catch a glimpse

(but we resisted had to run in front)
as of the bloom

(as he kept rotating away)
you've been staring at

(as the wind might do or the diamond)
half-fallen and some faint perfume still possible

(center of your life each time you look for it)
ouch-snag

(only this is it)
a quick thorn as you brush by

HOT SPRINGS CINQUAINS

If, when
    the young man rode
up on a pack horse with
cameras we had not just plunged
into

the hot
    pool then toweled
dry, gotten mountain chill
out of our bodies (two long-haired
waifs in

Big Sur
    eating seaweed
from a cup), we might have
agreed to undress dive neck-deep
into

the hot
    pool again at
dusk so we could be snapped
for National Geographic;
we were

not shy
    in our bodies
not even suspicious
of his invitation to be
in a

photo
    spread on hot springs
in the Northwest (who would
cook up such a story?). If we
weren't

so in-
  souciant in
love with our new sense of
female solitude—day's great climb,
full packs

and cramps
  up Ventana
Wilderness mountainside
sleeping out tentless we could hear
ghosts in

the wind
  of the vanished
Indians—we might have
agreed. As it was we shook our
damp heads

and lost
  the chance to be
two sleek seals in mountain
steam. Months later in a dentist's
waiting-

room I
  found the issue:
saw our hot springs—ghost of
our two heads—on the page. Twenty
years hence

finds me
  conjuring up
this picture for you of
our happy refusal to plunge
back in.

OBJECT MEMORY

Wear the cap (knitted chocolate brown)
and veer back
to an alpaca farm in the Negev
winter so you almost feel the wallaby nibble, claws
clutching your hand
full of seeds as it withdrew its ouch
and after, your lover withdrew

inside the whirlwind. Let the window
open onto a fossil field
you're being dragged back
to something and is everything you touch
unpurgable of this fog-tissue

so it sits in your palm
rides your sickbed-head, holds your
teacup with the neurons
folding you in folds? Take

the wood-carved loon so
newly still:
smaller than your pinky it rests on your desk
inside your unrest gathering
last summer's lakeside dust-

ups. Or that sponge you just scavenged
from the beach in St. Pete:

tiny   pocked   breath-holes   grey   soggy tube   hardened   in air—

already pipes the stroll with a petulant five-year-old.

Why else clasp on this silver bracelet
each morning like a talisman

plucked from inside a porcelain persimmon
your husband gifted you?

    Eight linked dime-sized coins embossed
with Chinese characters your dad brought back from
    San Francisco when you were twelve:

fú—lù—shòn—quán—vu—yi—jí—xiáng

    (Good Luck—Wealth—Longevity—Everything—
as You—Wish—Auspicious—Auspicious!).

        Aren't you triply pleased:
    by its resounding fortune,

    by the jingle the coins make
each time you shake your wrist,

    by the private song Memory makes
inside each uplifted thing?

VI

RIDING OUT A MONDAY AFTERNOON FUNK I READ CHARLES WRIGHT AND TU FU OVER A CUP OF GREEN TEA

steeping
           to give the right kick.

From the black sofa:
                    drone of roadwork
weatherworn water tower (my silo)
window view my only compass.
I'm itchy with lack of use
                    / the same as uselessness?

Late May. *Lament seizes every district.*
Tricornered irises in a water jar beginning to droop/fade.
Melancholic eye paints everything grey/blue
(no flooding here, drought eases after two days' rain).

Try to have each line prize
                         egg-cupped stillness before
lightning-rod telephone rings it away.

No harm recalling
                  early morning my son and I hand-in-hand
strolled to buy
one green-leafed cookie before bending
                         to sniff the rose garden's candied blooms

(my P'eng-lai tortoise holding up the world /
                              at least this day).

LETTER TO 700-YEAR-OLD INVIDIA IN THE SCROVEGNI CHAPEL
TO BE FOLDED IN THE SHAPE OF A SNAKE SWALLOWING ITS TAIL

                              . . . out of your niche, Galatea'd on hate,
if it weren't for the bloody anemonaed
flames (coelacanthed), that hold you phoenixed
rebirthed, recursed
    consuming you spewing you flue-ing
you up. Clutching your moneybag already
cinched
by the tasseled rope at your waist
    and reaching to grasp—what?—You can barely see
    for the serpent jutting from your mouth whose head circles
back to flick its tongue
over your eyes—your ears so outsized—batlike cartilage
    ram's horns wrap around.

    Embittered, Invidia,
what makes you so perdurable? Attractive in repulsion? The only
figure who rivets? Is it the things we cannot stand to see?
Or what we hear too strongly in the surround?
    I can barely keep writing
for want of
what others boast at the next table or blare into their cell phones (so many soliloquies
    of public preening that look as if the boulevard has become an open ward)
pounding
by me.

You too, I suspect, so self-consumed you've abandoned your stylus.
If you had to read the daily paper, your eyes would glare / bulge in despair
at all the accolades heaped
    upon your friends or those who do not stoop to know you—even to that one
Giotto

di Bondone has painted in stone across
       from you: Prudentia who calmly composes herself through the centuries
at her writing desk
                gazing with quill in hand at the mirror which soothes her
          feeds her new lines ignores you
          ouroboros you into a roiling frenzy

so done up in grisaille you practically leap . . .

BURN AND DODGE: A SONNET/GHAZAL

Too light? Too shadowed? For love, burn and dodge.
Can't imprint the face of ———? Spurn and lunge.

By rail to Devon-on-the-Sea; at the Dew Drop Inn
Played pool over ale; at the stove, bangers and mash.

Have you no concept of the worm? he harangued.
She frowned, smoked cigs of clove; Sturm und Drang.

Binocs in hand, stalked Lord God Bird in bayou woods;
Heard only other woodpeckers above fern and hedge.

Pour water from your boot, wine from your shoe.
At parties, skirt slit, curse Jove, flirt and fang.

Wind in the pines, cars stalled on the incline;
In summer, before you dove, stripped and dipped.

If your spirits snag on the heat's branch, fall;
Unwizen by cooling grove, wedlock and bedrock.

CURSED ANGER SING

Wound inside snake coils, cruel lover of blood
    who sees only red, unlike Gluttony, Lust,
and Sloth, when you are wroth,

can you delight in it? Like being possessed or obsessed,
    isn't Rage close kin to Envy because it flays itself
        as much as singeing its victim?

    Yet how can I hope to capture
    Wrath on the page when not in a froth
but in a reasoning calm? If Anger seized

me up, words would Kilauea—lava-erupt—
    then fall back to moil my stomach and snake
        up my shanked and coiled

    guts—and you would run. Must I demonstrate?
    Think how to behave when others rage at you:
Contract. Turn cool grey. Armadillo

your heart to the fury-darts being thrown at you, as I must do
    with my son. Ignorant teacher, he has taught me
        not to practice what he screeches;

    for I have seen Anger's ugly ruin boomerang:
    the heart burns, torn drawings, scratched
skin, hateful names that contort

the face of whoever flings them.

ON THE DEATH OF SOMEONE REVILED
(SCHADENFREUDE)

Sadder than when a friend or loved one dies
is the death of someone we despise:
with her fake Oxonian accent,
flip pronouncements on Classical art
and culture, her grey head shakes
to all we said, the too-red flush
to her skin that warned her heart
was pumping hard to circulate
her nicotine, her alcoholic wit,
and obscurantist erudition that shamed
those of us with our small-town
inflections or—heaven forefend—nasalities
from Brooklyn, which is where she ended up
living and dying after all she said.

PANDORA AND THE SUMMER AU PAIR

That you are her boss bemuses her,
reclining on the overnight flight, tucked
into her diary, disapproving of the balloon pants

you wear (*so dowdy, hiding her belly*). Upon landing:
haughty looks, hands forever on hips as though
about to launch into an aria of *I'm not really with them.*

Can anyone fail to admire her thick tresses spun
up with chopsticks against the Italian sun,
darkly cascading in the Riviera dusk, tight

Armani-sheened pants highlighting hips?
(*The kid I'm sitting for a complete brat
I do cartwheels for on the lawn: What form!*)

Has anyone ever *seen* such perfect skin before?
She thinks not. Watch her braid stray flowering
weeds into a garland for her hair. (*Some man*

has got to notice.) Outwardly cool, her yearnings
under cover, she barely speaks through dinner,
only rising to fetch the toddler. When she leaves

her diary lying under a chair in the boy's room,
how can you not open it? *She's the perfect
caricature of a doting Jewish mother my sister*

*and I would have laughed over. I cringe when she orders
the waiters in imperious Italian while her husband sits there
drinking quietly like a Buddha. Never mind. This afternoon*

*I met the Fiat tycoon—or is it Olivetti or Barilla pasta—
it hardly matters; He's invited me to Sardegna on his private
yacht! He's the kind of man—so rich and handsome who cares*

if he's my dad's age—I've always dreamed of meeting . . . Here
even you stop reading: embarrassed by the schoolgirl gush just as
she, terrified she's left the book and you might read of her disgust,

tries the lock—it's well past ten—hammers at the door.
Now who would have opened to that knock
instead of feeling affronted at being disturbed

at such an hour and crying, "Go away! You woke
us up!"—or admitted to reading it? And who
wouldn't have held such confidence like a lost key

in their back pocket while she's locked out,
reduced to waiting upstairs in her room—shaken,
insomniac—till morning to recover her spiral book.

Entering the breakfast room unrushed, you say, "Oh,
was this what you were missing?" holding it out. "Yes."
Profuse apologies for having knocked, she glances

up: the book returned over espresso cups
with a blank look confirms it unread.
You're wondering now why you didn't guess

when opened, her book becomes a box unleashing
Envy, Spite, Shame . . . and Hope? Half
carelessly that afternoon you leave your

notebook lying out (*It's better not to know
what others think of you*), half-expecting her to find it
and read of your transgression and regret—or else

half-hoping, someday, she might read this.

LICK-OVER

A lick over the foot doesn't qualify as a crime,
    though a cigarette butt or a soda can not thrown in a can
can in the Netherlands. But a flick over the boot: a man's
    still free to land however it might hypnotize, electrify, or outrage.
If you recline near the strand could you withstand a man's slobber—
    do you find it half-funny—a liquid wave from a landlubber (not your lover)—
or half-perverted? How else to word it: In the nick of a rudder in Rotterdam,
    some policeman's other gave not an utter damn
that the dames on the beach couldn't sunbathe—sleep—sweet and neat
    (Would a finger on a dyke have caused a louder rave?)
without this predator (not senator) slathering saliva on their feet.
    Would you go where the foam slipper-foes its toes? Lap of salt waves,
lip-lap, salty tongue on the run: what does it signify? The lawyers slow to meddle:
    What's to be done but make unsolicited toe-licking (a wettish fetish) illegal.

THE UNWRITTEN POEM

Was wearing four-inch heels and no makeup.

Fell out of a silver lamé clutch with a faulty clasp.

Has alligator eyes with invisible tears.

Only spoke itself as the express train roared by with you covering your
ears.

Asked for you repeatedly at back doors where you'd once lived.

And never lived.

Hates hats.

And sunlight.

And Nature.

Got chewed up in your mind by the black dog.

Scorned your best fountain pen, linen notebook, antique writing desk.

Favored the full lap, short subway rides, the fricative moment.

When chased by you, Daphne'd itself for months in Riverside Park.

Overheard one-way conversations and refused to fill you in.

Got invited to the party without you.

Slept inside an ellipsis.

Assented to all negations.

Developed an inferiority complex but would rather never live than ask
Fame to dance.

Made you believe you could capture it in Italy.

Fasted inside the waiting room of the still moment.

Refused to begin in medias res.

Gave up and distributed its letters into the dictionary.

Hid inside the dejà of vu.

Didn't like being talked about when out of the room.

Like your former friend who races by hoping you do not see her avoiding
you.

Was born a man who once had feelings for you.

Was the pulsing inside the silence.

Is in love with your ennui.

Is the ghost station that flashed by so only children caught it.

Feeds off your dolor.

Secretes itself inside your tea breaks.

Hates beginnings more than endings.
Has flat feet and refuses to walk too far.
Was last spotted whispering in the ear of your nemesis.
Would rather not be and not be asked the question.

OBSESSPOOL

paradelle

I try never to repeat myself.
I try never to repeat myself.
Do something new every day.
Do something new every day.
Do I repeat every day something
New never to try myself?

Two ducks make a paradox.
Two ducks make a paradox.
But go sneeze on goats' knees.
But go sneeze on goats' knees.
Go on a paradox knees; two ducks
Make goats sneeze but . . .

What does that have to do with it?
What does that have to do with it?
You ask. Everything and nothing.
You ask. Everything and nothing.
Ask that everything do nothing—
What? And with you? Does it have to

Ask goats nothing. Try and make
something sneeze: a duck's paradox.
Do you go on two knees?
I do—never every day—but what it
Does to myself with that new:
Have to repeat everything.

IMPATIENCE SCOLDING

> Perhaps there is only one cardinal sin: impatience. Because
> of impatience we were driven out, because of impatience we
> cannot return.
>
> —FRANZ KAFKA

Before the before / after
the before of the o'clock of heartbeat
to be late—belated—belabored urgency
of the rush to gather there is no time there is no yes

Before the after / then before you
awoke demanding on demand (the only sin
can't be bothered to wait for itself to)
Picture the blur of

       (How to record the too-slow-recording of the futility
       of capturing the impossibility of)

Why weren't you How could you
Before before It should have
I should have   You you always
day late life-
time short

       (Draw a picture—no—flip-
       book of getting up
       pacing unable to
       read straight through jumping up tumbling
       [motor speed of a six-year-old]
       push-honking
       never mind of turning
       away too slow
       to invite you back
       script illegible)

you will not be saved
because you fled before
the wingtip brushed
your face before
you refused to
fin

SIN-O-MINTS

she gifted you (she knew)
  what simmered inside:
    the horned grinning centaur
      shoveling more and more coals
        into the lickerish fire not just
          your private story but
            the billboard of the soul
              compressed to a round metal
                pillbox (cinnamon tabs snapped
                  in—the color of pencil erasers)
                    as though to ingest the flaming bits
                      could expel / release / or at least
                        erase the trace of what you spell (Diablerie)
                          inside / bathing in such forbidden flaming swamps:
                            supping Worry's stew, prone to Anxiety's flashes,
                              Anger's revels, and plagued by that chiefest of pests
                                roaring Despair Despond This Miry Slough stings
                                  you mid-December so uncased from your puparium
                                    you flicker, lucubrator, toward the bright-bulbed news
                                      that will burn you up.

EITHER / OR

1.

Hans Brinker or the Silver Skates: a tattered copy
for sale on the street to remind me of the conundrum of *or*:

Was it a matter of choosing Hans Brinker or the Silver Skates *or*
were these two possible titles? Or both? Maybe

I was stoned for the first time when I mused over
this semantic trifle, or maybe I wasn't. For

aren't our days packed with such parsings—light or ponder-
ous—and we can't always tell the difference: Did she mean

to snub me or was she similarly preoccupied?

2.

Conjunction of alternatives, Middle English *or*, earlier
other, auther, perhaps *either*. Early High German *er*

as in *earlier* or *before*. Of preference as in sooner rather
than later. As if one could choose. As if life hadn't already

chosen to set me at a standstill before

3.

                                        honeyed light-circle
the bare tree's branches in shadow against the stone wall

shimmer-lit or photographed—unfixed—that fixed me. Either way
it was the afternoon ore that had struck/mined me by chance

while strolling out of my building. I stood arrested. Was it a spot-
light from a building across the way (everything else lay in winter shade) or

the lucky happenstance of the sun raying between two buildings?
And why did this wavering shadow flung against a lit wall

stupefy me the way the real tree, barren, where no birds sing, never does?
I looked from one to the other: the silhouette or the winter tree itself.

They seemed to need each other the way I have often stood in my life in the middle
                                                                    of this

or that (or: a word to rift my heart) with awe. The mind loves choices while
the pendulous heart grows sick on them. Or does the heart love choices and the
                                                          mind . . .

Ordinary life: a husband and child or my panting solitude. I have made my choice.
But will I get to see branches lit up against stone once more or will memory's
                                                          flickering eye

have to cast tree-shadow against the wall as I go by? Should I have bought the copy
of the crumbling book or left it there or shall I go back for it today?

4.

Should I have let him come by the last night or not—though in my refusing him,
by accident he took his life? Would it have saved him
                                          or merely delayed him?

Are we fated to do what we do, or not? And if not, this either/or
makes me stumble and shake. Once, when my young life was about

to open, I stood before a mirror choosing between two coats—blue or green—
until I was doffing and donning them in a sweat-frenzied blue-green stripe. Then
                                                          between

candlesticks: Mediterranean blue or Venetian green. As though what covered me and how the light got thrown could ward off

5.

                                      all the other choices I could not make.

What if choices didn't require such gyrations of the soul, if instead they—gnarled branches, shadowed and raw—illumined each other. As if the ore inside the *or*

I err for could be found wherever I looked—as if I could finally gain entry into the land of *and*.

NOTES

The epigraph from Dante is my translation.

"Envy Speaks": The image in the first stanza is inspired by a Leonardo da Vinci drawing.

"The Truth of Poetry": The epigraph is from Marianne Moore's poem "Poetry," as it appears in Collected Poems of Marianne Moore (Faber, 1951).

"Current Events": Written in the aftermath of 9/11, this sequence of poems refers to some events reported in the New York Times during June 2002. The quote in "What-Knots" is taken from an article by Jane Perlez, September 17, 2002.

"Barbarous Thing": The opening sentence is from Amelia Roselli's poem "Irony an Even Harder Kneecap," translated from the Italian by Giuseppe Leporace and Deborah Woodard, published in Chelsea 72 (2002). The partial lines from Milton are from his "Sonnet XII. On the Detraction which followed upon my Writing Certain Treatises," the treatises being divorce tracts.

"At the Reception": Based on a photograph taken at a reception at the Library of Congress (1963).

"Ode to Fernando Pessoa": A homophonic poem based on Pessoa's "Triumphal Ode."

"Your Only Music": The opening line is from Keats's letter to his brothers, George and Thomas Keats, January 13, 1818.

"Clare-Hewn": This series of homophonic sonnets translates the English Romantic poet John Clare's sonnets, with their agrarian-based nineteenth-century vision and language, as though they had been written in a foreign tongue. The epigraph is taken from his sonnet "Summer Moods," where Clare himself "translates" birdcalls into human sounds.

"A Pact with Ezra Pound": Pound wrote, "What thou lovest well remains, the rest is dross" in Canto LXXXI of The Pisan Cantos.

"Envy Ghazaled": The epigraph is from Cervantes's Don Quixote, trans. Edith Grossman (2003).

"I Have": The epigraph is the opening stanza of Paul Celan's "Ich Habe Bambus Geschnitten," as translated by John Felstiner in Selected Poems and Prose of Paul Celan (2001).

"Hot Springs Cinquains": This poem is for Jody Rosenblatt Feld.

ACKNOWLEDGMENTS

With gratitude to the following journals and anthologies in which these poems first appeared:

American Letters & Commentary ("Letter to 700-Year-Old Invidia in the Scrovegni Chapel to Be Folded in the Shape of a Snake Swallowing Its Tail," "O Indigo," "Wanting Two: A Sonnet/Ghazal"); *Barrow Street* ("Be Where" [section 3 of "Current Events"], "Forms of Address," "No Ting," "Wrought Up by a Prating Son" [sections 3 and 9 of "Clare-Hewn"]); *Bat City Review* ("At the Reception, 1963"); *CHAIN* ("What-Knots" [section 2 of "Current Events"]); *Court Green* ("Burn and Dodge," "Sin-O-Mints"); *Crowd* ("They"); *Denver Quarterly* ("Her at Play," "Summer Moves" [sections 7 and 8 of "Clare-Hewn"] and "Uncentered @ Cathedral Rose Garden"); *Fiera Lingue* online ("Ode to Mrs. Meunier, Captain of the Guard, P.S. 119, Brooklyn"); *5 AM* ("On Not Being Lynn Emanuel"); *580 Split* ("Slatch"); *Georgia Review* ("The Unwritten Poem"); *Good Foot* ("Barbarous Thing," "Sonnet/Ghazal to Sleep"); *Jacket* online ("Door Litotes," "The Give, Seek, Am" [section 6 of "Clare-Hewn"], "Lick-Over," "Missed Hummer" [section 5 of "Clare-Hewn"], "Ode to Fernando Pessoa," "This Scabbard's Free" [section 10 of "Clare-Hewn"]); *Kenyon Review* ("Either/Or," "The Truth of Poetry"); *Laurel Review* ("An Ideal Lure" [section 4 of "Clare-Hewn"]); *Literary Imagination* ("To Guilt"); *Lyric Magazine* ("Tai Chi in Fog"); *Maggid* ("A Pact with Ezra Pound," "Passing"); *Natural Bridge* ("Ode to Turbulence"); *New American Writing* ("Be, As in Flotsam," "Tea Lay" [sections 1 and 2 of "Clare-Hewn"]); *New Republic* ("Regret," "The Want Room"); *Poetry East* ("Cloakroom Wit"); *Poetry International* ("Envy Speaks"); *Pool* ("Ghazal without the Man," "To the Family of the Man We Ate 130 Years Ago"); *Post Road* ("And How," "First Why" [sections 7 and 9 of "Current Events"]); *Prairie Schooner* ("Object Memory," "Ode to Ginger," "Pandora and the Summer Au Pair"); *Rattapallax* ("Grudge"); *RealPoetik* online ("Who You," "When, Then," "Why As In" [sections 1, 4, and 6 of "Current Events"]); *Runes* ("Cullet," "Shame"); *Whiskey Island Magazine* ("Envy Ghazaled," "Jealousy," "On the Death of Someone Reviled [Schadenfreude]"); *Women's Studies Quarterly* ("The Poem for Envy I Cannot Write")

"Obsesspool" appeared in *The Paradelle An Anthology*, ed. Theresa Welford (2006).

"Be, as in Flotsam," is included in *The Pip Gertrude Stein Awards in Innovative Poetry in English* (2006–2007), ed. Douglas Messerli (2008).

"Tea Lay" appeared in the *Best American Poetry 2007*, Heather McHugh, Guest Editor (2007).

"Envy Ghazaled" is included in *Letters to the World Poems from the Wom-Po Listserv*, ed. M. Richards, R. Starace, & L. Wheeler (2008).

"Entreaty to Indecision" was handprinted as a limited-edition letterpress chapbook by Delphi Basilicato (2006).

Thanks to *PoetryMagazine.com* for giving a second home online to "Uncentered @ the Cathedral Rose Garden," "Slatch," "Sonnet/Ghazal to Sleep," and "They" in 2003.

Thanks to *Poetry in Performance*, which reprinted "The Truth of Poetry" (Vol. 32) and "First Why" (Vol. 33).

Thanks to *Verse Daily* for featuring "The Truth of Poetry" in 2004 and "An Ideal Lure" in 2006.

Thanks to *Poetry Daily* for featuring "Letter to 700-Year-Old Invidia in the Scrovegni Chapel to Be Folded in the Shape of a Snake Swallowing Its Tail" in 2005.

"Lick-Over" was handprinted as a card by Delphi Basilicato to commemorate the Fifth Anniversary Reading of the Center Broadsides Reading Series (2006).

Abundant gratitude to Bob Hicok for taking my manuscript out of the darkroom and exposing it to the light. Thank you to Ed Ochester for his steadying advice and for giving my work a wonderful new home. And thanks to Supriya Bhatnagar for her enthusiastic support at the AWP. I want to express my enduring gratitude to all my friends who have believedin my work, especially Phillis Levin, Rachel Wetzsteon, Jeanne Marie Beaumont, Anna Rabinowitz, Jeff Friedman, and Cassandra Garbus for reading earlier drafts of this book. Also, heartfelt thanks to Barbara Leeds, Ellen Geist, Alfredo Rossi, Jan Bender, Amy Lipman, and Evan and Freda Eisenberg, whose abiding friendship sustains me through the light and the dark. And finally, to Sam and Sono, my dear loves, who bind me to the human and animal worlds.